An Unsolved Conspiracy

JACK COEY

Fulton Books
Meadville, PA

Published by Fulton Books 2024

ISBN 979-8-89427-679-3 (paperback)
ISBN 979-8-89427-680-9 (digital)

Printed in the United States of America

For my family.

It was the Gagnon boy at the door who said that Mr. Rich wanted to see me, and I was somewhat confused because I saw him first thing this morning, and things were routine. I thanked the boy, and he stood looking at the dials of the meters, which held curiosity for him. I watched him until he noticed me and ran off. I couldn't blame him; it is not often that an eight-year-old boy gets to look inside the waterworks. I finished reading and recording the meters and walked across the common to the bank, where Mr. Rich worked with my sister, Susan. I could tell from Susan's flushed face there was something going on. She was at the counter with Oscar Dillon. I went behind the counter and tapped on Mr. Rich's door.

"Yes."

I went in, and Mr. Rich was behind his desk like I'd seen him thousands of times before. He nodded for me to close the door.

"Can you drive me up to Dr. Dean's tonight, say, at eleven thirty?"

"Yes."

It was August 13, 1918, the last summer of the war.

I knew from dealing with Mr. Rich over the years that you didn't ask questions. He kept his feelings to himself, and he was a highly thought-out man in the town. He spent time in Concord in the House of Representatives and in the Senate. He was a municipal judge and had his own insurance business, was treasurer for the school and The Odd Fellows, and was a Mason too. He was a member of the New Hampshire National Guard. He was aloof and standoffish, but no one could say he wasn't distinguished. He graduated from one of those fancy colleges in Boston with a degree in engineering and thought he was smarter than everyone else—if he really wasn't. For me, he helped me a great deal with different jobs, and he got me into the Masons.

My current position as Superintendent of the Waterworks, he got for me, and that's not to say all he did for Susan. I tried to tell Susan he wouldn't leave his wife because he had too much to lose. She didn't like hearing that, but we knew it was true, but even so, she wouldn't break off with him. Maybe she figured going along with him was easier than having the tension of working together and being angry with each other. He was twenty years older than her and was some kind of father figure for her. We lost our dad when we were teenagers in a logging accident. Susan would leave the room when I asked her about Mr. Rich. The difference in my relationship with Mr. Rich is that I did chores for him, and he got me jobs, while Susan let him have his pleasure, but he did nothing for her.

Lately though, she started talking about Dr. Dean and how much fun he was and how he made her laugh. Dr. Dean and Mr. Rich and their wives had been friends for twenty years or so. The Deans lived on a hilltop farm two miles out of the village, and his wife suffered from senile dementia, so I could see how attention from Susan could fill a need for Dr. Dean. Dr. Dean was known to enjoy the presence of women, the younger, the better. The more I thought about it, the more I could see Susan maybe playing one man against the other. Not that Susan was calculating like that—she wasn't—but she was frustrated by Mr. Rich playing her along. Whatever it was, it looked like Mr. Rich wanted to talk to Dr. Dean about something.

And of course, people were worried about the lights from Mount Monadnock. It was August of 1918 in Jaffrey, New Hampshire, and hysterical people thought there were German spies on the mountain signaling boats in the ocean seventy miles away about troop movements from Fort Devens in Massachusetts. There was a man-made cave that men could live in that I had spent time in before the war. The Department of Justice sent two agents to Peterborough in April of 1918 to investigate espionage, and they talked to me a couple of times. I looked for lights, but I never saw any, though I knew a lot of people who said they did.

There was this suspicious couple renting a house from Dr. Dean who came from New York and had money named Colfelt, whom people thought was a German spy who had something to do with the lights. He didn't work or join the army. Old man Dean threw them off his farm in June of '18, saying he was too good an American to have people like that in his place. There was a rumor that Lawrence Colfelt was the illegitimate son of Johann Von Bernstorff, the German ambassador to the United States. Johann Von Bernstorff visited Dublin, New Hampshire, the next town over, twice during the summer of 1916. The Colfelts showed up in Jaffrey at the same time.

That was the summer when the Black Tom explosion happened in New Jersey. Munitions were blown up by German saboteurs that were being sent to England even though we were officially neutral. The summer of '16 was when people first saw lights from the mountain. Oh, there were certainly saboteurs working in this country; there's no denying that.

That night over beef stew, I told Susan about how Mr. Rich wanted me to drive him up to the Dean's place at around midnight. Old man Dean was an unconventional farmer who slept late in the morning and milked his cow late at night. He never had much money, and it was Mr. Rich who introduced Lawrence and Margaret Colfelt to Dr. Dean with the idea they rent the big house, and the Deans would move to the bungalow. Susan got flustered and red in the face and wouldn't look at me when I told her Mr. Rich wanted me to drive him to Dean's farm. Then I thought about how Tuesday was the night the stores and banks stayed open late so the farmers from the outlying fields could work late and still be able to do their shopping. Old man Dean came to the village on Tuesday nights and in all likelihood was in the bank and must have done something Mr. Rich didn't like. Whatever it was, my sister didn't want to talk about it.

I didn't go for that Colfelt chap much. Whenever he talked to me, he had a look on his face like there was a bad smell in his nostrils. He wasn't that way with Mr. Rich though, but Mr. Rich was a banker and Colfelt had money. Pete Hamill hired Ralph Davis and me to move Colfelt's stuff. It was the first week of June 1918, after Dr. Dean ejected the Colfelts from his farm. It took us two trips over to Temple and back.

The first trip was boxes and trunks, and one of the last items was this wooden box that Colfelt got fussy over. I went to move the box, and it was a dead ton. I asked Colfelt what was in it, and he said a victrola. Well, I scratched my head over that one because I've moved victrolas before and they don't weigh as much as this box did. I would say this box weighed four or five hundred pounds. Colfelt was a nuisance about keeping it upright and not juggling it too much. Colfelt may have thought he could pull one over on some country bumpkin, but I knew what people were saying about him, and so I figured it must be some signaling device. It took three of us giving all we got to get it on the truck, and when we were back in town. I said to Hamill, "Colfelt says that was a victrola."

Hamill laughed.

I met Mr. Rich at his barn at eleven thirty. I could tell he was angry, but I knew not to ask. Mr. Rich was one of those guys who let anger build up and up until it exploded. I'm sure that one of the reasons he was successful was he didn't let others know when he was angry. I got the buggy out and hitched the horse to the harness, and in silence, we drove the two miles to the Dean's place. The bungalow was on the left, and the barn was across a field, and the big house where the Colfelts stayed was further up. I stopped the buggy on the road, and he climbed down.

"Wait here," he said.

It was a warm night, and Dean's farm was elevated, and I could see the outline of Monadnock. I saw a kerosene light from the bungalow where Mrs. Dean was. I always liked her; she was very sweet. Seems like twenty minutes went by before through the darkness, came, "Russell…*Russell*…"

I didn't notice the black eye until the morning. It was obvious Dr. Dean clocked him a good one.

Mr. Rich looked at me from across his desk and said, "I hope I can count on your silence."

"Yes, Mr. Rich. It looks bad…it looks bad."

"I know, I know, but I have an alibi. I was kicked by my horse."

For the first time, I was disappointed with Mr. Rich, but I said nothing.

"We can say Mrs. Dean did it."

I was having a hard time with Mr. Rich, whom I always respected for his intelligence, being so silly. All I wanted to do was get out of his office.

"As a brother Mason, you are sworn to protect my secret."

"I know, Mr. Rich."

Mr. Rich looked at me for a long moment.

"I can count on your help, Russell."

"Of course, Mr. Rich, of course."

I left his office and never had so many conflicting feelings all at once.

Mr. Rich

Mrs. Dean didn't know what happened to her husband, and she was up most of the night hoping to see his lantern across the field. At daybreak, she went out to the barn, but couldn't find him. She went back to the bungalow and, at half past seven, heard a buggy come up the road. It was a young farmhand of Ingraham's, who was on loan to do some mowing for Dr. Dean—Arthur Smith—and with him was Ingraham's six-year-old son. He drove past the bungalow and out into a field where he stopped yesterday. He was unhitching his horse from the buggy to the mowing machine when he heard Mrs. Dean screaming. He looked up and saw her running across the field toward him. Arthur ran toward her, and when he got to her, she said, "I'm sure Mr. Dean is dead in the barn. Go look, go look, please."

Arthur went through the barn and found nothing. Arthur was outside deciding what to do next—he thought Dr. Dean had wandered off—when he heard a buggy on the road. It was Martin Garfield and his son, who Mrs. Dean called and told her husband went to the barn last night to milk the cow and never came back. The group of four walked the fields and ended up in the big house after trying all the windows and doors, and only found one unlocked. Martin climbed through the window and opened the door. The men and boys looked over both floors of the house quickly and came outside again. Garfield wanted to think things over, so he went and sat on the porch of the barn. After several minutes, the Ingraham boy came and sat with him just as Garfield saw some blood in the grass. The boy noticed it at the same time. The boy reached down and plucked a tuft of grass with blood on it, and said, "What do you call that?"

Garfield knew something bad happened, but he didn't want to scare the boys, so he said, "I guess Mr. Dean killed a chicken or something."

Garfield looked around him and saw blood on the stoop and spots on the door. He knew something bad had happened. He told the Ingraham boy he wanted to call down to the village, and he and the boy went back into the big house. He called William Coolidge, a selectman, and told him they were looking for Dr. Dean, who went to his barn last night and never came back. Mr. Coolidge got Mr.

Hogan, a selectman, and Pearly Enos, the acting chief of police, and Mr. Nute, the actual chief of police, and drove up to the farm. The group of four met the officials from the village by the side of the road.

The Barn

Martin told the men what they'd done, and it was Mr. Hogan who asked if they'd looked in the wells. Martin went with Mr. Hogan down to the well by the bungalow, and they took off the cover, and it was empty. Martin said, "There's a cistern by the big house."

They walked to the big house, and Pearly Enos and Mr. Coolidge were there. Mr. Coolidge took the cover off the well and asked for a stick of some kind, and Martin remembered a broom in the kitchen of the big house. Mr. Coolidge straddled the well, and when Martin handed him the broom, he plunged it into the water and stirred it around. He stopped still.

"I guess he's here all right."

The men were stunned. They looked at each other with disbelief. After a long moment, Coolidge said, "If you can get me a hook of some kind, I can hook onto him and pull him up."

Arthur Smith remembered an ice pick he saw hanging in the barn, and a car came up the road and parked. Charlie Stratton and Mutt Priest got out. They could tell something serious was happening. Coolidge saw Mrs. Dean coming up the road carrying a basket, and he guessed she wanted to feed the turkeys. He said, "You fellows look after this, and I'll go down and see Mrs. Dean doesn't come up here."

Arthur came with the ice pick and handed it to Charlie Stratton, who straddled the well and plunged the pick down into the well, and pulled up. They could see legs with rope wrapped around the knees.

"Let him back down," said Mr. Enos. "We can't move the body until the coroner is here. I'll go have Mr. Coolidge call."

Mr. Enos went off to the barn and told Mr. Coolidge. The two men walked to the bungalow, and Mr. Coolidge was about to make the call when a car parked across the road from the bungalow. Mr. Rich and his sister-in-law, Georgiana Hodgkins, and William Leighton, the undertaker, got out, and Coolidge thought, *"Why is there an undertaker when no one knows he's dead yet?"*

The men saw the black eye. It was like seeing a black eye on a priest or teacher. Mr. Rich behaved as if nothing was out of sorts, and the men out of respect, didn't call attention to it. Garfield and Mr. Rich were standing by the well, and Mr. Rich said, "Looks like a case of suicide."

"If you have any doubts about it, if you think a man could do it tied up that way, we'll pull him up to the top of the water and let you see."

"I don't care to see him," said Mr. Rich, and he walked off toward the barn.

It was probably an hour and a half before the auto-carrying Roy Pickard, the county attorney, and Dr. Dinsmoor, the county coroner, drove up the road. The sky was darkening with a coming storm. The men gathered around the opening of the well and Mr. Coolidge repeated his operation, and when the legs appeared, Mr. Hogan wrapped his arms around them and pulled the body out of the well.

The body was tied in four places, his ankles, his knees, and his hands were tied behind his back. There was a burlap bag over Dr. Dean's head with something inside it and a rope around his neck. It was a grisly sight. The men stood over the body and looked down like it was the carcass of an animal they'd never seen before. They could see there was something in the burlap bag. Mr. Coolidge took out a pocket knife and slit the burlap bag and a medium-sized stone fell out. There was the sound of thunder in the distance, and Dr. Dinsmoor said, "Let's move him into the house."

The Dean House (Built in 1983)

Arthur Smith took him under the arms, and Charlie Stratton by the ankles, and they carried him into the sitting room of the big house. It was decided by Dr. Dinsmoor and Roy Pickard to move him to Leighton's Funeral Parlor to examine the body. A heavy rain and booming thunder started. The rain got so heavy that it washed away much of the outside evidence.

On the day Dr. Dean was murdered, he and his wife were visited by three women, one of whom was Mrs. Morison of Peterborough. The women were asking for donations for a rummage sale to raise money to build a hospital in Peterborough. Mrs. Dean came to the screen door, and Mrs. Morison noticed food stains on her dress. Mrs. Dean thought they were religious people, and Mrs. Morison had to explain more than once who they were and what they wanted. Mrs. Dean pushed open the screen door to let them in. They stood awkwardly in the sitting room until they heard footsteps on the stairs, and Dr. Dean came into the room. Mrs. Morison had the impression he was starting his day, which was late for a farmer. When talking to three women, he turned on the charm and listened closely as Mrs. Morison explained why they were there. He said, "I would like to give you a good big check, but I can't afford to, but if there is anything in this room you want, take it."

Mrs. Morison was a close observer of the lights on the mountain and helped bring the Department of Justice to Peterborough in April of 1918. Dr. Dean offered some books from his bookshelf, and Mrs. Morison suggested some antiques, which seemed to strike an idea in Dr. Dean. He said, "I haven't any here, but over at the other house, I have a few. If you will come over with me, perhaps you can find something that would interest you."

Mrs. Morison saw that her two companions wanted to stay with Mrs. Dean, so she walked with Dr. Dean to the big house. They went into the sitting room and looked around, and saw nothing. Dr. Dean said, "If you wait here a moment, I'll go upstairs to get a spinning wheel which you might like."

It wasn't but a few minutes before Dr. Dean came back down with the spinning wheel. They started out of the house and were about halfway across the field to the bungalow when Dr. Dean stopped and said, "Mrs. Morison, Miss Ware told me that you had seen lights up in this part of the country. Have you seen them lately?"

"Yes, Mr. Dean, I saw them last night."

"About what time?"

"I would say a little after twelve."

"I wonder if you could show me from where? Do I get the same view as you do? Could you show me the place where they came from, from here?"

"Yes, I can show you the exact spot."

Mrs. Morison walked a little further in the field until she had a good view of Monadnock.

"It's a great pity I can't see Monadnock from my house," she said.

Dr. Dean didn't respond. When Mrs. Morison looked at him, he appeared to be thinking about something. She waited for him to speak.

"Mrs. Morison, are you ever in communication with anyone who could be of any help with the lights?"

"Yes, I am in constant communication with the Department of Justice in Boston."

"Can you do something for me?"

"Yes, I'd be very glad to."

"Can you get a message to send me up one of the very best agents they have? I want the very best, not just an ordinary man who doesn't know his work."

"Mr. Dean, couldn't I do more than that? Couldn't you tell me what it is, and I will get the message to them at once? I'll telephone as soon as I get home."

"No. I don't want you to telephone. I can't give you the message because what I know is too dangerous for a woman. I have no right to tell you."

"Why, Mr. Dean, if it is so serious as that, why haven't you sent for someone before?"

"Because I wasn't ready. Two agents were over here last spring, but I wasn't ready. I wanted to be perfectly sure. Now the quicker someone comes, the better."

They walked in silence. Suddenly, Dr. Dean stopped and asked, "What do you know about the Colfelts?"

"Why, I don't know anything about them. I think you know more than anyone else as they are living on your place."

"I did, Mrs. Morison. I knew just a little too much. I gave them twenty-four hours to get out."

"What do you mean, Mr. Dean? What was the matter?"

"Well, I needed the rent very much, but I'm too good an American to keep people of that kind on my place."

They were at the bungalow, and Mrs. Morison held the screen door for Dr. Dean.

Susan came to get me at the waterworks and said Charles wanted to see me. It was Thursday morning, the day *The Peterborough Transcript* was published. I closed the door behind me.

"Have you seen *The Transcript?*

"Not until lunch."

"Can't wait that long. Let me read it to you, "In the barn nearby there were some blood stains, and there were others on the piazza of the house."

I started to move toward the door.

"I'll take care of it."

I rode up to the farm and shoveled some manure from the barn and wiped away some blood spots from the floor and wall and went up to the big house and wiped up some blood from the porch and the sink in the kitchen. Not long after that, a Department of Justice agent showed up at the waterworks and asked me who sent me to the farm to clean up. I said, "No one."

"Why did you do it?"

"I was turning off the water so the pipes wouldn't freeze."

"In August?"

I felt dumb but didn't say anymore.

Mr. Rich, his wife Lana, Georgiana, his sister-in-law, and Susan believed Mrs. Dean killed her husband. They said she killed him in a jealous rage. She was still on the farm, two miles out of town, with police and nurses to look after her. Mr. Rich went to the selectmen and asked that she be sent to a sanitarium for a mental evaluation, which would be less expensive to the town and better for Mrs. Dean.

Dr. Dean was buried on Saturday the seventeenth, with no autopsy. The following Tuesday, Oscar Dillon, Miss Hiller, Mrs. Bryant, Dr. Childs, and a nurse came to the bungalow and told Mrs. Dean they wanted to take her on an automobile ride. Mrs. Dean refused. Mrs. Bryant tried to coax her, Oscar Dillon tried to coax her, and at last, Dr. Childs told the nurse to give her a hypodermic needle. She was groggy, and they got her in the back seat of the auto, and drove her to the Herbert Hall Sanitarium in Worcester, Massachusetts. The next day, I was called to Mrs. Bryant's house for a pipe leak, and when I finished the job, we were talking about nothing in particular when I mentioned there was a theory going around that Mrs. Dean killed her husband in a jealous rage. I didn't know she had taken Mrs. Dean to the sanitarium the day before.

"This talk that Mrs. Dean killed her husband is absolute foolishness. She is incapable of that kind of violence. But there is talk from the Rich household about her killing her husband, and the Riches and the Deans were such good friends for so many years that I marvel at what people can say about each other. Mrs. Rich warned me about Mrs. Dean—not to be alone with her—she might be the murderess. We moved Mrs. Dean to the hospital in Worcester yesterday, and I must say plainly, I'm ashamed of my part in this. Mr. Coolidge told me and Miss Hiller to help Dr. Childs.

"Mr. Coolidge said it was costing the town money for police and nurses, and they wanted to see if she was insane or not. She's no more insane than I am. She's forgetful and absent-minded, yes, but insane? Not on your life. Somebody wants her out of the way so they can say what they want about her. She is a kind and gentle woman, and what people say about her, especially people who profess to be her friends, will make your blood run cold. Dr. Childs was in charge, and he told me to have Miss Hiller help me because we were forcing Mrs. Dean to do something against her will, and she could be difficult.

"I tried to make it as easy as I could; I tried to coax her. I kind of suggested to Mrs. Dean she might like to take an automobile ride with us. She wanted no part of that, so when it became obvious, we were going to have to be forceful, Dr. Childs gave Miss Hiller a hypodermic needle with a sedative. She snuck up behind her, and injected Mrs. Dean. Very shortly, Mrs. Dean began to get drowsy. Her face flushed, which worried me, and she said, 'What if I died now? You wouldn't need to come over anymore. You have been awfully good to come here every night and stay with me.'

"We helped Mrs. Dean out to the auto and got her in the back seat—Miss Hiller on one side, and me on the other. Mr. Dillon drove. Dr. Childs followed us to Jaffrey, where he turned off, and we drove on to Massachusetts. Mrs. Dean would nod off and wake again, complaining about being tired. She kept asking if we were taking her back to her farm. I lied and told her we were taking a roundabout way. I feel terrible about this. I'm ashamed of myself for deceiving a vulnerable, trusting woman like that. I would feel the same way about lying to a child. She was getting more and more agitated about not being at home when something funny happened. I started to hum, and she said, 'I didn't know you could sing,' and calmed right down.

"It was funny how my humming calmed her down even more than the sedative. When we arrived at the asylum in Worcester, she got out of the auto and wanted to know what time it was. I told her it was half past three, and she said, 'We have been going for a long time. I am going to rest awhile, and then, we will start home again.'

"Mrs. Dean had no idea what was going on. We got her in a chair in the waiting room, and when she closed her eyes, the three of us got out of there as fast as we could. I felt so bad I felt like crying. We played an awfully dirty trick on that woman, and the poor dear had just lost her husband. The selectmen tried to tell me it was for the best, but I didn't feel good about it when we did it, and I don't feel any better talking to you right now. I realized after that she could have stayed with me in Jaffrey, but of course, I always think of the better plan when it's too late."

I felt bad for her and tried hard to think of something to make her feel better, but I couldn't, so I said, "I'm sorry, Mrs. Bryant," and picked up my tools and left.

What Mrs. Bryant told me haunted me for some time. We were tools in a power system we couldn't afford to challenge. My respect for Mr. Rich was not what it was, but it was not just Mr. Rich either. Like Mrs. Bryant, that helplessness didn't feel good.

On Friday night, the twenty-third, two couples got off the four o'clock train from Boston, and one of the couples I recognized was Dean's brother, who lived in New York City. The other couple looked like they came from Paris. I was on the platform picking up some freight. The man was short, and very handsome, well-dressed in a dark suit, and he wore a monocle. They were sophisticated—or to me they were. She was plain but dressed in bright colors with crazy patterns on her dress, it seemed like, to distract from her plainness. Dean's brother recognized me, so I went over and introduced myself. He told me his name was Frederick.

"Welcome to Jaffrey," I said, "I'm sorry about the circumstances."

"Well, I hope Dr. Dekerlor can help us find out what happened."

I shook the short man's hand, and he had a look on his face like I was a bad smell.

"This is my wife, Elsa Schiaparelli."

I went to extend my hand, but she nodded her head as if touching me would give her some disease. I felt like taking back my welcome.

"If there's anything I can do to be helpful, please let me know."

I picked up my package and left.

Susan had the same feelings about Dekerlor as I did. They came into the bank to see Mr. Rich the following morning; Fred Dean, because of his earlier visits to see his brother, knew Mr. Rich was the man to talk to. Dekerlor was one of those guys who rubbed people the wrong way. Mr. Rich told Susan he didn't like Dekerlor, not for a second, and Dekerlor, after one look at Mr. Rich and his discolored face, became suspicious. Dekerlor was an outsider with no investment in the town, and that put Mr. Rich on edge. The more Dekerlor looked at Mr. Rich, the more suspicious he became. Mr. Rich told the men about the murder, how the body was found in the well, and how he was tied up with a sack over his head.

Mr. Rich said how there were gashes on his forehead. Placing his monocle in his eye, Dekerlor asked how many gashes there were. Mr. Rich answered three. Dekerlor wanted to know how they would get there, and Mr. Rich talked about the three-pronged cultivator found in the barn, which it was believed Dr. Dean was struck. Then the detective wanted to know how long the scratches were, and Mr. Rich, with tension in his voice, answered an inch and a half. The two men played thrust and parry with Frederick Dean nervously watching. He knew Charles Rich well enough to know he did not like having to answer to others. Dekerlor finally made a lunge and said, "It looks like you got quite a whack on your face."

Mr. Rich stiffened in his chair. Mr. Rich in a terse voice, told how after supper his wife gave him a basket of pea shells to feed the horse, and because of the fresh sawdust on the barn floor that muted his entry, he startled the horse, and she kicked out. The kick hit the basket, which knocked the pipe he was smoking up into his eye. Mr. Rich stopped talking, and there was silence. Dr. Dekerlor had a smirk on his face. Mr. Rich, perhaps to deflect the conversation away from his eye, talked about how Mrs. Dean was the suspect, how she was alone with him, and how she was moved to a sanitarium in Worcester to evaluate her mental state and keep her safe.

Dr. Dean loved women, especially young women, and that, said Mr. Rich, caused Mrs. Dean to be jealous. That got Frederick Dean involved in the discussion. He and his sister-in-law did not get along—she didn't tolerate his drinking—but even with that, Frederick knew his sister-in-law was a kind and gentle woman. Frederick decided to end the interview. When they were out of the bank, Dekerlor said, "Well, how can a horse kick a man's face and make a cut here, and a cut there? The whole side of his face would be smashed. Looks more like a fist than a hoof to me. Let's go look at the crime scene, shall we?"

That afternoon, the two men rented an auto from Hamill's garage and drove up to Dean's farm. They got out by the bungalow and walked over to the barn. Dr. Dekerlor had a magnifying glass. He began looking over the barn porch and stairs. Frederick looked at the mountain and remembered how majestic it was. After several minutes, Dekerlor asked, "Where's the well?"

Frederick didn't know for sure but took him up to the big house, and it didn't take them long to find it. Dekerlor bent over and examined it with the magnifying glass. He stood erect and proclaimed, "I have a hypothesis!"

"Really?"

"Yes. You see, I saw the scratch marks on Mr. Rich's face which, if they correspond to the scratch marks I've found on the barn porch, and here on the foundation of the big house, and with the scratch mark on the victim, wouldn't that place Mr. Rich at the scene of the crime?"

"Okay, but how are you going to get the scratch mark from my brother if he's buried?"

"Exhume him."

"I thought you could talk to the dead. Wouldn't that be easier?"

"Communing with the victim of a violent death is difficult."

"Oh?"

Frederick Dean knew enough about small New England towns to know that asking permission to exhume a body would be difficult. Besides, he didn't want to dig up his brother. He dropped by the bank and asked Mr. Rich about what to do, and Mr. Rich was perturbed at the idea but told Frederick they would have to get permission from the selectmen.

On Monday morning, Dr. Dekerlor and Frederick Dean met with the selectmen. The Dekerlors had attracted attention in a small town of farmers and factory workers. The selectmen were uncomfortable with strangers, foreign strangers more than that, and foreign strangers who were doctors even more than that. On top of that was the suspicion that Dekerlor was after Mr. Rich. The three selectmen were at one end of a long table and Federick and Dekerlor at the other. Frederick spoke first, "Gentlemen, thank you for seeing us this morning. May I introduce Dr. Willie Wendt Dekerlor who's here to help me investigate my brother's murder. Dr. Dekerlor is the vice president of the International Congress for Experimental Psychology, the author of several books, and a correspondent for *The New York World* and *The Boston American.*"

The selectmen watched Dekerlor like an alien from another planet and slowly nodded.

"Dr. Dekerlor has completed a preliminary examination of the murder scene and has gathered evidence that leads us to make the following request. We ask permission to exhume my brother's body—"

"What?" Peter Hogan cried out.

Dr. Dekerlor opened his mouth to speak, but Coolidge grabbed the attention.

"Gentlemen, gentlemen, gentlemen, before we go any further, I would like an opportunity to talk with our visitor and get to know him better. It is unusual for us to have such a distinguished visitor in our town. Good morning, Doctor."

"Good morning."

"I hope you're finding the village of Jaffrey friendly, sir."

"*Quaint* might be the word."

"Yes, I see. What is your occupation?"

"I am a psychologist—a criminal psychologist—and a doctor and lecturer."

"Very good. When you say doctor, do you mean physician?"

"Doctor of Philosophy."

"Interesting. Where are you from, sir?"

"My wife is a fashion designer and instructs others in the occult, so we reside in Paris, and have an apartment in Greenwich Village as well."

Coolidge chuckled, and the two other selectmen, after catching on, chuckled too.

"My, you must find New Hampshire boring."

Dr. Dekerlor removed the monocle from his eye.

"Quaint, like I said, but I gave my word to my friend that I would help him uncover the circumstances of his brother's death."

"How do you know Frederick Dean?"

"We are lecturers in Manhattan. Same circuit, different topics, however."

The room was silent until Boynton asked, "You speak more than one language?"

"Yes, I speak five languages. I speak German and French best of all. I speak English, Polish, and Italian next best, and Spanish afterward. I have studied about eighteen other languages also. I can read them, but I don't speak them much. I know some Russian. I travel extensively, and am very well-known, not only in New York, Washington, and in France, as well as England and Italy, but I am very well-known probably all over the world through my various writings and my various activities."

There was silence as the selectmen tried to grasp the genius at the other end of the table.

"Your English is good," said Hogan. The two other selectmen slowly turned and looked at him.

"You want to exhume Dr. Dean's body?" asked Coolidge.

"Yes," answered Frederick Dean. "Dr. Dekerlor has—"

"If I may, sir," interrupted Dekerlor, putting his monocle in his eye. "You see, I have measurements taken at the crime scene which, when I match them to the scratches on an individual's face, will place that individual at the crime scene."

"Remarkable," said Boynton.

"But for me to be reliable, I need the marks from the victim's forehead."

The selectmen didn't like the sound of that, and there was silence until Coolidge spoke, "Well, I would ask we adjourn this meeting until after lunch, which will allow the selectmen time to consider your sensitive request. We would have to consider the family—"

BOSTON SUNDAY POST

DE KERLOR'S "PSYCHIC PICTURES" IN A N. H. MURDER MYSTERY

Was it a German spy who mysteriously killed William K. Dean at East Jaffrey, N. H., last August?

This is the story of extraordinary detective work.

It might read like fiction at first—the deductions are as fine as those of Sherlock Holmes in their uncanny shrewdness. But Dr. William de Kerlor is one of the noted psychologists of the world, a member of scientific organizations and an author of repute.

The Sunday Post is able today to give, for the first time anywhere, his remarkable deductions that would show how the mysterious murder at East Jaffrey, New Hampshire, was committed last August.

BY RELMAN GREENE

"Mrs. Dean is in Worcester," interjected Frederick Dean.

"This meeting is adjourned until one o'clock," stated Coolidge.

The selectmen adjourned for half an hour for a quick lunch and reassembled in the conference room. Coolidge stood at a window and looked down on Frederick Dean and Dr. Dekerlor on the street below. He heard a voice in the background, turned from the window, and realized it was Boynton talking.

"Just tell him while we respect—or maybe even admire—his expertise, this is a town matter, and has to be dealt with by town authorities."

Hogan agreed, saying, "We don't want an outsider like that poking around in our town business. Which of us has not benefitted from a favor from Charles?"

Coolidge sat at a desk with his head in his hands, and forcefully said, "You're overlooking something."

The two selectmen looked at Coolidge.

"What?" Hogan asked.

Coolidge dropped his hands and brought his head up.

"The man writes for two major newspapers. He could make us the laughingstock of the country."

There was a pause.

"No, gentlemen, I think we let him have his way."

"But Bill, he's going to make trouble for Charles," said Boynton. "We all know Charles can rub people the wrong way, especially people that don't know him."

"I agree, Ed, but there's nothing we can do about that. This exhuming the body is a crackpot idea, and if we make a stipulation that we have to be present to observe his findings, then all we have to do is claim that his findings were inconclusive, and this whole trick will go nowhere."

"But what if he is conclusive?" posed Hogan.

"You're going to prove murder with scratch marks?" challenged Boynton.

"Maybe so, but he's trying to put Charles at the crime scene," said Coolidge.

"If this doctor is so world-renowned and accomplished, what's he doing in Jaffrey?" asked Hogan.

"It's a chance to make himself famous," said Coolidge.

There were two Department of Justice agents, Feri Weiss and Robert Valkenburgh, who were in Jaffrey investigating the lights. Because of Dr. Dean's conversation with Mrs. Morison about the lights, and he was murdered later that day, there was the possibility that the murder was an act of espionage to keep Dr. Dean from telling what he knew about the lights. The Masons were angry when they heard about the exhumation of Dean's body; it was clear Dr. Dekerlor was trying to implicate Mr. Rich. Nobody trusted what Dekerlor was up to. It came to light that before joining the Department of Justice, Feri Weiss had been an immigration officer in New York Harbor and knew about the Dekerlors.

He went to Roy Pickard, in the county attorney's office in Keene, and told him the background of the Dekerlors. They had been deported from England in 1915 for sorcery and attending Bolshevik meetings. Roy Pickard, who believed Mrs. Dean killed her husband, thought that if Frederick Dean knew this, maybe he would go back to New York and take Dekerlor with him. He dispatched Sheriff Lord to Jaffrey to ask Frederick Dean to come to Keene for a meeting. At the time of the meeting, Frederick and Dekerlor showed up at the Keene Jail, and the sheriffs were annoyed with Dekerlor and led him to a holding cell while Frederick went into the sheriff's office. Roy Pickard was standing behind the desk and pointed to a chair. Frederick sat.

"This man you're traveling with, how well do you know him?"

Frederick shifted his weight.

"He and I lecture on the same circuit in New York. I've known him for six months or more. Our wives are friends; Mrs. Dekerlor is a talented fashion designer."

"Do you know the Dekerlors are being followed by the British Secret Service for their participation in the Communist Party?"

"Ah, no."

"Do you know the Dekerlors were deported from England in 1915 for cheating people out of their money for occult activities?"

Frederick Dean got red in the face.

"I didn't know that."

"I would caution you, Mr. Dean, to be cautious in your association with him. He's more dangerous than you think."

"Of course."

"Besides which, the investigation is focused on Mary Dean, who we believe killed your brother in a jealous rage."

Frederick Dean looked puzzled.

"Well, Mr. Pickard, I don't know about that. Mary and I never liked each other, but even with all that, I don't believe she's capable of that kind of violence."

"I understand your sentiments, Mr. Dean, but you don't know how much her mind may have deteriorated from the last time you saw her."

"I still don't believe it."

Pickard, annoyedly looked at Frederick Dean for several beats, and then said, "But the more pressing problem is your association with Dr. Dekerlor, and I want to encourage you to go back to New York and take him with you. You can see we have enough around here as it is, and the last thing we need is an outsider who doesn't understand the people and how we live, to get mixed up in the middle of it."

Frederick Dean gave out a small smile.

"Oh, I don't know if I have much influence over Dr. Dekerlor. I'll try if you ask me to, but I can't promise. He's pretty eccentric."

"I understand," said Pickard.

The following morning, Dr. Dekerlor noticed Frederick Dean was quiet. He was too good of a detective not to have suspicions after Dean's interview with Roy Pickard. When Frederick did speak, it justified the doctor's suspicions.

"We're not getting anywhere; we should go back to New York."

Dr. Dekerlor stopped walking.

"What! Mr. Dean?"

"They don't want us here. We're only interfering. We should go back to Manhattan."

"And leave your brother's murder unsolved? That would be an insult to his memory."

"Don't you see? There are forces at work here of which we are not a part."

"My dear Mr. Dean, you're allowing yourself to be intimidated by small-town activities that should be nothing to you."

"Are you calling me a coward?"

"Mr. Dean, I don't back down from a threat, and you shouldn't either. For the sake of your brother, if nothing else."

"I'm leaving on this afternoon's train, and you should come with me."

"Absolutely not. I said I would investigate this, and I won't be put off."

"They know about you, Doctor, and they will use your Communist sympathies to destroy you."

"Ha! Hardly. My politics don't rise to the gravity of murder."

Frederick Dean walked away from Dr. Dekerlor and left Jaffrey that afternoon.

With the abandonment of Frederick Dean, Dr. Dekerlor had to make some money, and a week later, this ad appeared in *The Peterborough Transcript*:

"World Renowned Clairvoyant and Palmist, Dr. Willie Wendt Dekerlor, is available for palm and tea readings at the Granite State Hotel, Room 302, from three to five o'clock, Wednesday afternoons. Fees Negotiated. *The Future is in the palm of your hand.*"

Two married women, Adele Johnson and Edith Foster, came to the door and knocked. Edith slipped her wedding band off her finger. The door opened, and there stood Dr. Dekerlor, short but handsome in his black suit. He slightly bowed and motioned the women in. The shades were drawn, and the room was lit by candles. There was a table with a crystal ball in the middle of the room.

"How can I be of assistance this afternoon, ladies?" purred Dekerlor.

The women smelled incense. Dekerlor pointed to a chair at the table and brought another. He placed his monocle in his eye and studied the women.

"I would like my palm read, and maybe some clairvoyance after," said Adele.

"Hmmm…yes, I see," said the doctor, "Clairvoyance is for the living and the future, and a medium communes with the dead and past."

"I want to talk with Martha Washington," blurted out Edith.

Dekerlor chuckled.

"I'm afraid it doesn't work that way. You see, you must have some corporal connection to the person you're communing with."

"Oh!" exclaimed Edith.

"I would like you to predict my future," Adele asked.

"All right, then, close your eyes and concentrate. Your hand, please."

Adele hesitated and then gave him her hand. Edith giggled.

"Shhh!" hissed the doctor.

Edith blushed. Dekerlor moved his thumbs over Adele's palm while looking at the ceiling.

"I see three children," he pronounced.

"That ain't right!" exclaimed Edith.

"Two. A boy and a girl."

"That's not right either," said Adele. Edith giggled.

"Quiet, please! You're interfering with my concentration."

Dekerlor let out a sigh and refocused his concentration.

"I see one child."

"Brilliant!" exclaimed Edith.

"There's negative energy in the room that is interfering with my ability to read accurately."

"I bet there's no interference when it comes time to pay the bill," observed Edith.

"Your child is a boy," said Dekerlor.

"Wrong again."

"I see the number forty-five," offered Dekerlor.

"I don't know what that is," said Adele.

"Your age, perhaps?"

"Wrong again!" snapped Edith, "you charge people money for this?"

Dekerlor gave Edith a dirty look.

"There's too much negative energy in the room."

"Try me then," suggested Edith, extending her hand, palm up.

"Of course, mademoiselle."

"Ha!" exclaimed Edith as she pulled her wedding ring from her pocket.

The selectmen gave Dr. Dekerlor permission to exhume Dr. Dean's body. It was at the end of August when the men gathered at the headstone, which read: *William K. Dean, 1855–1918.* The selectmen were there—William Coolidge, Peter Hogan, and Edward Boynton—and the town undertaker, Mr. Leighton, Reverend Enslin, and the doctors, Childs and Dinsmoor, an angry-looking Mr. Rich, Charlie Nute, Chief of Police, and the Master of Ceremonies, Dr. Dekerlor.

Dr. Dekerlor believed in photography as a crime-solving device and asked Mr. Johnson, who was the owner of the photography store in Jaffrey, to come and take photos of the deceased. Mr. Johnson was setting up his tripod and camera and some men were pulling the casket from the ground with straps. Once the casket was out of the ground, Mr. Leighton wiped off the dirt. Mr. Coolidge stepped forward and said, "Gentlemen, may we bow our heads."

The men removed hats and bowed their heads while Reverend Enslin recited a prayer. After he said, "Amen," the men stirred.

Mr. Leighton went to the coffin and loosened the top with a hammer and pry bar. When the corpse was revealed, several men stepped back. Several of the men moved out of Mr. Johnson's way so he could take photographs. He took a photo, moved the tripod, adjusted the angle of the camera, took another photo, and repeated it again. He nodded his head, he was satisfied. Dr Dinsmoor and Childs did a quick examination of the body, and when they finished, Dr. Dekerlor approached the casket with a sheet of white paper and a pencil. The men who looked saw a gash mark on the crown of Dr. Dean's head. Dr. Dekerlor bent over and carefully traced the gash mark onto the sheet of paper. When he straightened up, he said, "Gentlemen, if you would be so kind as to meet me at the Dean's farm."

A half-hour later, the men gathered at the barn, and Dr. Dekerlor, with his magnifying glass examined the porch and said, "Gentlemen, I've found in three different locations scratch marks from the garden cultivator, which, if I can match to a fourth location, will place that individual at the scene of the crime."

None of the men looked at Mr. Rich, and the tension was intense.

"Marked on my paper—which you observed me do—are the scratch marks from the victim's forehead, which should match these marks in the barn porch."

He bent over and applied his paper to the marks on the porch, and several men bent over too to see if they matched. The men murmured assent. Dr. Dekerlor marched the group up to the big house and looked at the foundation of the house above the well.

"The third set of scratch marks are here in the foundation."

The men, taking turns, looked at the paper covering the scratch marks and saw a match. Dr. Dekerlor walked over to Mr. Rich and placed the paper over his face and said, "Strange to relate, these marks on the paper fit the marks on Rich's face. Mr. Rich, tell us, where did you get your black eye?"

The men froze.

"At the right time and place, I will tell," answered Rich.

No one in Jaffrey would dare accuse Mr. Rich of murder, and an outsider making the accusation infuriated the Masons. With Mrs. Dean buried away in a sanitarium in Massachusetts, the official line was she killed her husband, and Mr. Rich got his black eye from a horse kick at nine o'clock. There was this fellow, Albany Pelletier, who worked as a night watchman at Bean & Symonds, the lumber yard, and I knew him to be a simple, honest fellow. Jaffrey, like many towns, was divided between Catholic and Protestant. The Masons did not allow Catholics to join, and the Protestant owners and managers, me and Mr. Rich included, were in the Masons. Albany witnessed something that did not match the version of events given by Mr. Rich and Ed Baldwin, his neighbor. I think Albany also knew that given his place in Jaffrey society, no one would listen to what he knew. Late on a humid night, not being able to sleep, Albany went to see Father Hennon to ask for advice. As he approached the rectory, he saw a single window lit. He knocked at the door and waited. He hoped Father Hennon was up reading, and he felt uneasy having him get out of bed. He was about to knock again when the door swung open, and the housekeeper holding a candle stood there.

Father Hennon

27

"Is Father Hennon available?"

"One moment."

The light receded down the hallway, and after several moments, came back again.

"Come in," she said.

He entered the door and followed the woman down the hallway. She knocked on the door before opening it and guided him into a room where Father Hennon was reading. She left the room, closing the door behind her, and Father Hennon took off his glasses. He was a handsome man with receding black hair and a well-proportioned face.

"Albany," he said, "this is unexpected."

"I know, Father, and I'm sorry to disturb you like this. There is something weighing on me, and I don't want another restless night. I hate to disturb you at this late hour, but I know I won't be able to sleep until I can share this with someone."

"I see," said the priest, motioning Albany to a chair. "You couldn't share this burden with your wife?"

"I have, Father, but I need to tell someone in authority."

Father Hennon smiled.

"Albany, I don't know how much corporeal authority I have."

"I need some guidance as to what to do," Albany earnestly said.

"I see. Tell me what's troubling you, and I'll see if I can help."

They heard a rumble of thunder in the distance.

"Father, on the night of the murder, I saw Charles Rich's horse and buggy at the Bean & Symonds sawdust chute at nine o'clock."

The two men made eye contact.

"I don't think I understand," said the priest.

Albany leaned forward in his chair.

"Rich is telling everyone he was kicked in his barn right before nine; he swears to it. How can it be if I saw what I saw?"

The men heard the clap of thunder.

"Oh, yes, yes indeed, I see your problem. You saw Charles Rich at the sawdust chute?"

"No, no, Father, it was Ed Baldwin, but it was Rich's horse and buggy. That I know for sure."

"Why would Ed Baldwin be driving Rich's horse and buggy?"

"They share a barn, and sometimes Baldwin comes to the chute for bags of sawdust."

"With Rich's horse and buggy?"

"Yes, Father."

"You're certain of this?"

"Yes, Father, I am."

There was a loud clap of thunder. In the silence after, Albany asked, "What should I do, Father?"

The priest stood up and walked to a window, and looked out for several moments, before he said, "Albany, as difficult as this is, I'm glad you shared your burden with me. The authorities should be notified of what you saw. What were you doing at Bean & Symonds at nine o'clock in the evening?"

"I was the watchman that night. I was making my nine o'clock rounds, and that's when I saw Ed Baldwin at the chute. I was fired a week after when I told my supervisor about what I'd seen. He claimed I was sleeping on the job, which wasn't true."

"No wonder you can't sleep."

"Rich has a lot of influence in this town, and I know if I say anything, it will bring me trouble."

"You're doing the right thing, Albany, and the problem now is who do we talk to, so we won't be ignored? I think our best chances are with the Federal men."

"You cross those town guys, and it makes it hard to get a job."

"I understand, Albany."

There was a peal of thunder.

"Sounds like I'm going to get wet," joked Albany.

The distrust and suspicion between the Catholics and Protestants in town was made worse when Father Hennon gave Dr. Dekerlor a room at the rectory house. Dr. Dekerlor was desperate for attention and got the keys to the big house on the farm where the Colfelts lived, and the following day was in the lobby of the Granite State Hotel off the common, telling passersby he had new evidence in the Dean murder, and it didn't take long for a crowd to gather. As usual, Dr. Dekerlor made people angry—this time, the hotel manager, who was a Mason. Dekerlor was holding a cardboard box, and he announced, "Gentlemen, I have been investigating the buildings on Dean's farm and am pleased to announce l have found important, new evidence that I feel will explain why Dr. Dean was murdered."

He held the cardboard box in the air.

"Inside this cardboard box, which I found in the former residence of the Colfelts, contains fifty or so postcards made up from photographs taken by Colfelt's daughter for her college friends. Seemingly innocent postcards—until you examine them more closely. All fifty postcards contain the same objects, but it is the order of how the objects are arranged that becomes significant."

He sat the box on a chair and held up a single postcard.

"This postcard, which can be made up at any photographer's shop, was made up from a photo negative of Colfelt's daughter. In this postcard, you will see various, and apparently random, objects on the mantelpiece. You will please observe the objects on the mantelpiece are a toy dog, a stuffed teddy bear, a child's doll, and a clock. A seemingly innocent postcard, gentlemen—until you begin to go through all fifty or so of the postcards, and then, you will observe the significance of the postcards."

He took his monocle from his eye and spun it, flashing light around the room.

"What you will observe upon further examination is that the order, or sequence, of the objects on the mantelpiece, changes every eighth postcard or so, and I submit to you, gentlemen, that this is a code used by the Germans to communicate intelligence."

The men murmured.

"At every eighth postcard in this box, the order of the objects on the mantelpiece changes, and the position of the hands on the clock changes in each postcard, and I say to you, gentlemen, that the objects on the mantelpiece represent constellations in the northern sky, and the hands on the clock tell the time the signals are to be sent. Each object on the mantelpiece represents a constellation. The toy dog represents the constellation Canis Major, and the stuffed teddy bear represents the constellation Ursa Major, and the child's doll represents the constellation Perseus."

Dekerlor replaced his monocle.

"I am European and know how clever the Germans are with astronomy. When I discovered these postcards in the former residence of the Colfelts, I saw through their ruse and interpreted them as a code of some kind. Further examination of my theory reveals these three constellations form a forty-five-degree triangle in the northern sky, which the Germans use to communicate their messages. If you examine it, you see the bear constellation is on the left, the child constellation is at the apex, and the dog constellation is on the right. There's your forty-five-degree triangle. Now those three constellations are the positions in the sky where the lights are to be flashed, which gives the message, and the hands on the clock give the time the messages are to be sent."

Dekerlor paused to give his audience a moment to assimilate his brilliance.

"Now if the first signal light is flashed at the apex of the triangle—or the child—and the second signal light flashes to the right, or the dog, and the third goes to the left, or the bear, that would be one message. The direction of the light goes from right to left. To change the direction of the signal lights in the sky, the spies change the order of the objects on the mantelpiece in the postcard. Like I said, the order of the objects in the postcard changes every eighth postcard to change the direction of the signals in the sky. If the child is first, then the bear, and finally the dog, the lights go from left to right, and then back to the child. They're using the same forty-five-degree triangle, but the direction the signal light travels changes the message."

A tall farmer asked, "What you're telling us is if the first signal is at the apex of this triangle you're talking about, and the second signal is to the right, and the final one is to the left, the message would be—let's say, Boston, right?"

"Yes."

"All right, then. If the first signal is the apex, and the second signal is to the left, and the last signal is to the right, the message would be different, something like, say, Portsmouth?"

"Exactly. The Germans use the same triangle and change the message by going left to right or right to left. They could even use multiple flashes in the three positions to have more messages."

A man holding a notebook, and pencil asked, "The signals are flashed from Monadnock?"

"I've been told there's a cave near the summit which would give them shelter."

The man wrote in his notebook, and then, asked, "Do you think this guy—the tenant on Dean's farm, Colfelt—was signaling, and Dean was on to him?"

"These postcards prove that."

"Some people are angry with you for accusing Rich," observed the reporter.

"Mr. Rich is a banker, and Colfelt is wealthy enough not to work, so the idea that they are confederates is not out of the question."

"You think both men killed Dean?"

"Why does that surprise you? Good day, gentlemen," said Dekerlor

The investigation moved slowly. Roy Pickard, the county attorney, told anyone who asked that Mrs. Dean was the primary suspect, and she was in a sanitarium in Worcester. Because of the possibility that Dr. Dean was murdered to keep him from talking to Department of Justice agents, two agents, Robert Valkenburgh and Feri Weiss, were staying at Mrs. Morison's farm in Peterborough. Mrs. Morison was a fervent believer in the signal lights. There was a story about how she saw signal lights and called up Charles Bass, the former governor of New Hampshire, who came to her house with two other men, and watched for the lights with her.

She pointed to lights in the sky, and Mr. Bass saw it was the constellation Sirius and told her so, but she was not to be dissuaded. Father Hennon began talking with Valkenburgh and Weiss about convening a grand jury after being convinced Albany Pelletier was telling the truth about Rich's horse and buggy being at the sawdust chute at nine o'clock. When Roy Pickard was asked about it, he answered there wasn't enough evidence to justify it, and he reiterated his belief that Mrs. Dean killed her husband.

Valkenburgh and Weiss suspected Roy Pickard of not pursuing the investigation with much vigor and learned that he'd been appointed county prosecutor when the man elected couldn't continue. This opened the possibility that Pickard owed a favor. Pickard was a small-time Republican lawyer in Keene until he was chosen to be county attorney. Mr. Rich spent time in state government in the House and Senate and knew a significant number of powerful people. For Valkenburgh and Weiss, that presented the possibility for Pickard that helping Mr. Rich was helping himself.

Lawrence and Margaret Colfelt came to Jaffrey in the summer of 1916. Johann Von Bernstorff, the German ambassador to the US, made two trips to Dublin, New Hampshire, the next town over, and held meetings in a cabin in the woods. People saw lights from the mountain, the summit of which is the first land sighting sailors see from the ocean. In July, German agents blew up a munitions depot in New York Harbor, destroying millions of dollars of munitions that were to be sent to England. Enemy espionage wasn't taken seriously in this country, with the Atlantic Ocean separating us from Europe. Because of his wealth, Lawrence Colfelt was conspicuous in a small New England farming town, and it didn't take long for Mr. Rich and Colfelt to meet.

The Colfelts went back to New York at the end of the summer of 1916 and showed up again in August of 1917. Mr. Rich was aware of Dr. Dean's ongoing problem with money, and, he suggested that the Deans move to the bungalow on the farm and rent the big house to the Colfelts. That arrangement was made, and the Colfelts spent the winter of 1917–18 on the farm, which people thought unusual. It was an unhappy arrangement from the start. The Colfelts lived off a trust fund, and so Colfelt neither worked nor joined the army which certainly didn't go unnoticed by the locals. Colfelt didn't help himself with his haughty attitude toward the farmers and villagers.

Predictably, whispers about Colfelt being a German spy started, which were fueled by Colfelt riding his horse or driving his touring car around the countryside. It was said that Colfelt was the illegitimate son of Bernstorff. Given Colfelt's unearned wealth and Dr. Dean's constant worrying over money, a conflict was unavoidable.

The rupture came the first week of June when Dr. Dean evicted the Colfelts from his farm "because I'm too good an American to keep people of that kind on my place."

The Colfelts moved to a hilltop house in Greenville, and on the day of the murder, Colfelt was working at the Atlantic Shipbuilding Company in Portsmouth as a laborer making forty-two cents an hour while staying at The Rockingham Hotel, which at his pay from his job alone, he couldn't afford to have his shoes shined. He started his job the Monday before Dr. Dean's murder on Tuesday. It was a two-and-a-half or three-hour drive from Portsmouth to Jaffrey, but on the night of the murder, Mrs. Morison reported a vehicle going by her house at a high rate of speed about eleven thirty or quarter to midnight and coming back, still at a fast speed, at quarter past one. This was unusual at night on a country dirt road lined with trees, without any lights on.

Mr. Rich said that Dr. Dean visited him at his home the night Dean was murdered, and that was contradicted by witnesses who saw Dr. Dean going back toward his farm at the time Mr. Rich said he was at his house. Mr. Rich wanted people to know there was no hostility between him and Dr. Dean. According to Mr. Rich, Dr. Dean came to his house after the kick by his horse. Georgiana Hodgkins, who was Rich's sister-in-law, was visiting from Long Island was the third person to know how Mr. Rich got his black eye, along with her sister, Lana.

Georgiana was a school teacher in Manhattan, and Valkenburg and Weiss thought it was a good idea to give her a surprise interview. They took the train from Boston to New York and went to the Washington Irving High School, and the principal was surprised to learn why they were there and to whom they wanted to talk. He led the men to an empty classroom, and several minutes later, there was a knock on the door. Georgiana came in, her face pale, and her eyes darting around the room.

"Please have a seat," offered Valkenburgh.

She sat at a student desk, not looking at either man.

"I'm Agent Valkenburgh, and this is Agent Weiss from the Department of Justice. I assume you know why we're here."

Georgiana coughed and took a moment to compose herself.

"Yes," she whispered.

Valkenburgh asked her how Mr. Rich got his black eye. Between her coughing and whispery voice, Valkenburgh had to ask several times to repeat herself.

"Did Dr. Dean visit Mr. Rich the night he was murdered?"

"Yes."

"Are you positive that Mr. Rich had a black eye and bruised face at the time of Dr. Dean's visit? Mr. Rich said Dr. Dean visited him right after he was kicked by his horse."

"Yes."

"What did Mr. Rich say as to how he got his black eye?"

"He said he went in the barn, where the horse was eating, and when he put his hand on her, she kicked out, and hit him in the face, which knocked his pipe into his eye."

Weiss asked, "What time did this happen?"

"Right around nine o'clock."

"What was he carrying?"

"I don't know."

She had a spasm of coughing, and Valkenburgh offered her a handkerchief, which she declined.

Valkenburgh asked, "Did you talk it over with Mr. and Mrs. Rich in reference to what to say when anyone would ask you?"

"Positively no."

"Your answers are the same as Mrs. Rich's," accused Weiss.

"That's because we have been talking about it between us, which is only natural."

Valkenburgh asked, "How did Mr. Rich hear of the murder of Dean?"

"Some rumor from the village."

"Are you sure Mr. and Mrs. Rich didn't receive word over the telephone?"

"I'm sure they didn't receive word over the telephone."

"Then the records in the telephone office calling Rich's house from Dean's house are wrong?"

Georgiana had a fit of coughing. She said, "I wish I could talk more, but I have such a very bad cold. I hope Mr. Rich won't be mixed up in this—for, you know, circumstantial evidence is very bad. Mr. Rich appeared the next day with a black eye. You know Dr. Dean saw the black eye when he was at Mr. Rich's house, but he is dead, and there is no one else except the family to prove he had a black eye."

"That is a problem, isn't it? commented Weiss. "Especially since Mrs. Dean testified her husband was back on the farm when Rich said he was at Rich's house."

"And she was the last one to see him alive…"

"Presuming no one came onto the farm," said Valkenburgh.

Georgiana coughed so badly that she excused herself.

Dr. Dekerlor knew he was being watched by the Department of Justice for his involvement with the Communist Party, and particularly by Feri Weiss because of his background in immigration. He knew Weiss must have provided the information to Roy Pickard that got Frederick Dean to abandon him to leave for New York. Dr. Dekerlor looked up Feri Weiss's address in the Boston phone book and made several trips to Cambridge to stake out his house. He thought if he could get into Weiss's house and see what reports he had on him, he would have a better idea of where he stood with the Department of Justice.

According to Miriam, Feri's wife, this is what she told her husband, "It was a Sunday night when I came home with Lillian, and I had a funny sensation like someone was here. Then I saw the muddy footprints on the carpet. I took Lillian upstairs with me, locked our bedroom door, and barricaded it with a chair. She fell asleep, thank God. I lay down on the bed next to her. I lay there in the dark, and I was almost certain there was someone in the hall when I heard the chain for the electric light being pulled, and I saw the light under the door.

I slowly got up and went to the bureau, took out a revolver, and dropped the holster, which made a noise. I was terrified. I heard a noise from Lillian's room, and then the sound of a window being opened. I went over and looked out our bedroom window. I saw

Dekerlor run along the roof, then crouch down, and jump from the roof. When I was sure he was gone, I checked the house and saw the papers on your desk were tampered with and thought he must have been looking for some reports. Feri, I came within a heartbeat of shooting him."

Father Hennon went before the selectmen to ask for a grand jury, and they were polite but noncommittal. They told him Roy Pickard, as county attorney, would have to order that. Father Hennon knew Roy Pickard was inflexible in his belief that Mrs. Dean killed her husband. He knew he wouldn't get any support from the Masons. About a year ago, Mr. Rich and Father Hennon had a disagreement that caused Father Hennon to withdraw the church funds from Mr. Rich's bank.

On Tuesday mornings, an altar boy brought the deposit from the previous Sunday's collection, and when Mr. Rich counted the deposit, it was eight dollars less than what Father Hennon counted. Mr. Rich insulted the altar boy and Father Hennon by insinuating the altar boy took the money. Father Hennon trusted the altar boy, and so an accusation against the altar boy was an accusation against Father Hennon. The Masons and Roy Pickard were opposed to a grand jury, again saying Mrs. Dean was the leading suspect. The Masons didn't want a grand jury because they believed it would railroad Mr. Rich to indictment and that Father Hennon was after revenge from the deposit incident.

The Department of Justice promoted the idea of an autopsy, which meant exhuming Dr. Dean's body for the second time. The Department of Justice hired Dr. George McGrath from Harvard to perform the autopsy, which was scheduled for January 1919. Valkenburgh and Weiss hoped that an autopsy would provide evidence that would discount the Mrs. Dean Killed Her Husband Theory.

On January 1, 1919, John Bartlett became the governor of New Hampshire. He was a Republican and a Mason. His attorney general, Oscar Young, was also a Republican and Mason. Mr. Rich knew both men from his time in Concord. Father Hennon, seeing that the grand jury request was going nowhere, started a petition among the townspeople to present to the governor requesting a grand jury be convened.

On a bitterly cold day in January, soldiers from Fort Devens arrived at the Conant Cemetery to dig Dr. Dean's casket out of the cement-like ground. After an hour and a half of backbreaking work, the soldiers carried the casket into the receiving tomb and waited for the officials. At two o'clock, Valkenburgh and Weiss, the selectmen, and Mr. Leighton, the undertaker, arrived at the receiving tomb to watch Dr. Magrath perform an autopsy. One of the selectmen brought a small oil heater to offset the cold.

Dr Magrath handed out oil-scented handkerchiefs to the men, which they quickly used when the top of the casket came off, and a stench filled the tomb. Valkenburgh and Weiss helped Dr. Magrath lift the partially decomposed body of Dr. Dean out of the casket and lay it on a wooden platform. Dr. Magrath removed the coat and shirt. He looked over the body. He took out a saw to cut open the skull and held Dr. Dean's head like a football. When he began to see, the head slipped from his grasp because of the fluid on the head. Feri Weiss took the head in his hands and held it while Dr. Magrath sawed. As the doctor sawed, fluid splashed up onto Weiss's face. Valkenburgh took out his handkerchief and wiped Weiss's face. When Dr. Magrath made an incision in the skull, he stuck his finger in. After examining the skull, Dr. Magrath asked that the body be turned over which Weiss helped him do. After he was finished, the agents helped him return the body to the casket.

For Valkenburgh and Weiss, the results of the autopsy changed the direction of the investigation. Dr. Magrath found Dr. Dean's skull was cracked and his neck broken, and for a sixty-six-year-old woman with dementia to accomplish that much force on her husband, in addition to dressing the body with a blanket and ropes and carrying the body a hundred and fifty feet up a slight hill and dropping it into a cistern in darkness, was ridiculous. The agents knew that promoting Mrs. Dean was a decoy. They wanted verification from a medical man, and they took the train to Worcester to interview the superintendent of the Herbert Hall Sanitarium, Dr. Chase.

When Valkenburgh read the autopsy findings to Dr. Chase, he said, "Doesn't surprise me."

"That's what we thought too," answered Weiss.

"Mrs. Dean is not capable of that kind of violence, neither physically nor temperamentally. I have spent much time observing and evaluating Mrs. Dean, and it is a total physical impossibility for her to have murdered her husband the way he was murdered."

"More like two men, I should think," suggested Valkenburgh.

"Yes, that makes more sense," agreed the doctor, "or one very angry man."

The more the investigation went on with no progress other than Mrs. Dean being the suspect, the more unsettled the town became. The murder worsened the distrust between the Catholics and Protestants, with the Catholics suspicious of Charles Rich and the Protestants sympathetic to Mr. Rich. The Grange, in an attempt to bring forth the latest information on the crime, invited Roy Pickard and Dr. Dekerlor to speak at their January meeting. Roy Pickard spoke first and said how Mrs. Dean was the only person on the farm when her husband was murdered, how her husband had a lustful nature, and how she was jealous of his flirting with other women.

Roy Pickard was told by Lawrence Colfelt how Dr. Dean mistreated his wife, which was contradictory to how the townspeople knew them. Publicly, they were a loving couple, but according to Colfelt, privately, Dr. Dean ate steak while his wife ate bread, and he criticized her for her lack of coherence from her dementia. That was the reason Dean wanted them off his farm—because they saw things that were embarrassing to him. Between her husband dallying with women and mistreating her, Mrs. Dean had plenty of reason to kill her husband, concluded Pickard.

Dr. Dekerlor walked to the podium. He took his monocle out of his eye and said, "Gentlemen, it is my pleasure to report to you the most startling discovery I made from taking photographs of the crime scene. I took photographs of the barn porch where Dr. Dean was attacked, and bloodstains were found. Later on, in my studio, as I developed the negatives, there was nothing out of the ordinary until I saw a small, whitish formation on the negative. I looked at it more closely, and amazingly saw a man's face. When I looked further, three other faces appeared, one of them a woman."

A puzzled murmur came from the audience. Roy Pickard, in the business of challenging witnesses, couldn't restrain himself.

"Can you show us the photograph? I'm certain we're all most curious to see the photograph," Pickard challenged.

"I'm afraid not. It's with a psychic colleague in Boston."

"Of course, of course, you make an exorbitant claim with no evidence!" exclaimed Pickard.

"I didn't know I would be asked to speak tonight until after the photograph was mailed," shot back the doctor.

"It is against my better judgment to ask this question without any way to prove your answer, but whose face did you see in the negative?

"Charles Rich."

"Just as I thought. And that was the only face you recognized?"

"There was another face, but it revealed itself only to one who has extrasensory powers."

Roy Pickard smirked. "Would you be willing to share that information with those of us who are reality-bound?"

"The lawyer, Mr. Smith."

"Reginald Smith of Boston?"

"Yes, that's correct."

Pickard turned to the audience. "How can that be? Reginald Smith didn't know anything about the murder until after it happened."

"Your ignorance is that you don't comprehend metaphysics. This is something that is known only to the very few. I would suggest there are various categories of thinkers—there are thinkers who are within the bounds of the philosophical, and others who go into metaphysics—still, others are, perhaps, more advanced than either, who, besides having a metaphysical understanding, have a metaphysical vision."

"Metaphysical vision? Metaphysical vision!" boomed Pickard. "Who in God's name knows what metaphysical vision is?"

Pickard paused and stared at his audience for emphasis. "I don't quite understand you, sir," he continued. "Let me see if I can make this more understandable to those of us who don't have a metaphysical vision. The reason why Charles Rich's face appeared in the negative was because he was there when the bloodstains, which were part of the negative, were made. Have I got that right?"

"Yes, that's correct."

"So how can it be that Lawyer Smith's face would be in the negative when he didn't even learn about the murder until a considerable time after it happened? He wasn't there when the photograph was taken."

"Those of us in the occult know this to be a prophetic picture, a prophetic projection of the event."

Pickard paced back and forth. "You mean to say the negative that was developed from the bloodstains on the porch, put there at the commission of the murder, prophesied the future connection of Mr. Smith to that murder?"

"I would say that in reality, all the lives of men form but a very small link in the bigger chain of cosmic events, and I would say, in the life of man, the future is nothing but the past unfolded. That is to say, we reap what we have sown. And if in the consciousness of man, which is made up of his past and future, and in his blood as an electric charge, could attach itself to negative plates, such faces that appear on those plates would be acknowledgments, or perhaps, projections of future events."

Pickard was still a statute. "So in essence, you can predict the future?"

"I would say so, if we understand, we have access to our destiny."

"Sounds to me like what we shovel out of a stall. You say there was a woman's face?"

"Yes."

"It was not Mrs. Dean."

"Whose was it, then?"

"I didn't recognize the face."

"Then how do you know it wasn't Mrs. Dean?"

"Because it was a younger face."

"So you could make out a face, but couldn't recognize it?"

"Yes."

"Maybe it was a prophetic projection?" sneered Pickard.

"Or maybe it was Susan Henchman."

Pickard was angry at himself for being outfoxed.

The idea started when Father Hennon told Valkenburgh about the incident with Delcie Bean. Delcie Bean and Merrill Symonds owned the lumber yard in Jaffrey where Albany Pelletier saw Charles Rich's horse and buggy the night of the murder. The incident was over a newborn and baptism. The Catholic Church decreed newborns should be baptized within the first two weeks of life. When Mrs. Bean had their baby, Delcie was in the north woods lumbering, and the couple got to the church later than the two-week stricture. Father Hennon criticized the couple for their lateness. That made Delcie Bean angry, and he left the church.

Father Hennon said, "Delcie Bean is a proud man who doesn't take criticism well."

Over supper that night, Valkenburgh relayed the story to Weiss, and he thought for several moments before saying, "Bob, I think this could be an opening for us. Father Hennon is right, men like Delcie Bean are proud, and see themselves as community leaders who sacrifice for the community. Any suggestion that they engage in any illegal or immoral act is an insult to their reputation and character. That's why the Masons are a secret organization—to protect the upstanding character of its members. The Masons don't want a grand jury hearing because of Rich's vulnerability to indictment. I bet if we looked at the signatures on the petition, we wouldn't find Bean or Symonds. If I'm right about that, there's our hook. We show up unannounced and push the men on why they haven't signed the petition, strongly suggesting they are protecting Rich—purposely pressuring Mr. Bean to get him to overreact and reveal something."

Valkenburgh thought about that, *We should get Clifford.*

"Good idea," agreed Weiss, "he's just the man to make Bean and Symonds feel like criminals."

"I'll send him a telegram," offered Valkenburgh.

Norman Gifford was the assistant superintendent of the Boston office of the Department of Justice, and he had a reputation for tough-nosed interrogation that compelled suspects to say more than they wanted. His nickname was "The Nutcracker."

The following morning, the agents went into Duncan's Drugstore and looked over the petition. Bean and Symonds were not on it. Later that day, Valkenburgh got a return telegram from Gifford saying he would be on the early train from Boston, which would give them time to go to Bean and Symonds in the early afternoon. On Friday morning, March 21, Valkenburgh and Weiss met Norman Gifford at the train, and as they had lunch at the diner, Valkenburgh told Gifford how the autopsy eliminated Mrs. Dean as a suspect, further exposing Rich. He told the story of their trip to the sanitarium in Worcester and how he'd asked Mrs. Dean to carry a chair across the common room and how she had to put it down four times before she got it to him.

In the early afternoon of March 21, the three agents showed up at Bean & Symonds and identified themselves to the young girl behind the desk, and asked to see Bean and Symonds. She asked if they had an appointment, and when they told her no, she offered to make one for them, to which Gifford told her they would happily get a search warrant and go through the facility, or they could keep this quiet. The girl stood up and went into one of the offices. She came out, followed by a man who introduced himself as Delcie Bean. Gifford told him who they were and what they wanted. Mr. Bean disappeared for a moment and came back with his partner.

They separated. Norman Gifford went with Delcie Bean into his office, and Valkenburgh and Weiss went with Symonds into his office. Every twenty minutes, either Valkenburgh or Weiss would switch and join Gifford to keep Bean and Symonds off guard. The Federal men pushed hard on Bean and Symonds to protect Rich, and Bean and Symonds were unaccustomed to being spoken to in this way, and the session got tense fast. Gifford didn't back down, and Bean and Symonds were angry. When Gifford knew he had the men where he wanted them, he called the session over but told Bean and Symonds if need be, they would be back again, and that the session was confidential. As they were leaving the building, Gifford said, "The water's boiling, gentlemen, the water's boiling."

The federal agents weren't Delcie Bean's only problem that day. Later that night, his nine-year-old son developed a fever, and he called for Mrs. Bryant to care for him. Through a partially opened door, she heard an angry Delcie Bean ask the operator for Roy Pickard and demand they meet in a Winchendon hotel room the following afternoon. Mrs. Bryant was angry at the men and how they treated the innocent Mrs. Dean. She struggled about saying something to the Federal men, and on Saturday morning, the desk clerk handed a note to Valkenburgh that she wanted to see them right away. Valkenburgh walked over to the infirmary, and Mrs. Bryant told him about the secret meeting that afternoon in a Winchendon hotel room. Valkenburgh was delighted that Weiss's strategy worked as it was supposed to. Valkenburgh walked back to the hotel and found Weiss reading the paper in the lobby. Weiss, too, was thrilled his plan worked.

When the time came, Valkenburgh and Weiss got in their auto and drove to Winchendon. They identified themselves to the clerks at the two Winchendon hotels, and it was at the second that the clerk said he had a two o'clock reservation for the "Rotary" of Jaffrey. Valkenburgh and Weiss asked the clerk to rent them the room next to the "Rotary," which he did. When the men got to the room, they were pleased to find a door separating the rooms, which would make it easier to listen to what the men were saying. Valkenburgh took a glass from the dresser. Weiss went down to the lobby and sat behind a newspaper to watch who came in. Right around two o'clock, Delcie Bean and Merrill Symonds came in and asked for the room number from the clerk, and climbed the stairs. Several minutes later, Homer White and William Webster came in and asked for the room number, and climbed the stairs. After an interval, Roy Pickard and Sheriff Lord entered and asked for the room number, and climbed the stairs. After several more minutes, Weiss went back to the room and watched as Valkenburgh listened through the door. Weiss could hear raised voices. After about twenty minutes, the meeting broke up, and after Weiss and Valkenburgh heard the last of the footsteps on the stairs, Valkenburgh sat on a bed and reported, "I couldn't hear all of it, depending on volume and the direction of the speaker, but

I got the gist of what Delcie Bean wanted. He told Pickard to go to Concord and meet with Oscar Young, the state attorney general, and get permission to convene a grand jury that would hear witnesses but come to no indictment. That way, Rich can claim exoneration, and the federal guys have no reason to hound Rich's supporters."

"Why would Oscar Young agree to that?"

"I'm guessing Oscar Young is a Mason, and I know the governor is a Mason, and Rich has spent time in Concord, so he knows who owes what favor to whom. Rich is a Mason as well, so there's that angle."

"I'll go to the library and look up biographical information on all the players to see if there's a connection."

It was about a week later that Roy Pickard announced a county grand jury after months of saying there wasn't enough evidence. It would run from April 11 to April 22 at the Keene Courthouse. Feri Weiss had another idea, and it was to petition the judge, John Kivel, to allow a federal attorney to assist the county and state attorneys in the proceeding in the event the murder of Dean was an act of sabotage and came under The Espionage Act of 1917, so the lawyers wouldn't have to duplicate the evidence already given. Father Hennon was concerned Albany Pelletier would be overlooked because what he saw contradicted Rich's assertion he was kicked at nine o'clock. Valkenburgh and Weiss made an appointment to meet with Judge Kivel in his chambers. They were joined by Father Hennon and the selectmen of Jaffrey. Feri Weiss went first.

"Your Honor, in the event of a Federal Grand Jury on espionage matters, and the possibility of Dr. Dean's murder being an act of espionage, would you grant a federal attorney to assist the county and state attorneys to prevent unnecessary duplication?"

"No. Motion denied."

Judge Kivel recognized Father Hennon.

"Your Honor, there is a member of my parish who saw something that contradicts what Mr. Rich has said about the night of the murder, and I would ask that he not be overlooked in the proceeding."

"Very well. If you give his name to the clerk, I'll pass it on to the lawyers."

"If I may, your Honor, I too would ask for a Feder—"

"Motion denied."

The judge recognized William Coolidge, a selectman. He didn't get very far when the judge cut him off.

"The state of New Hampshire doesn't need any help from outsiders. Good day, gentlemen."

When Valkenburgh and Weiss were on the sidewalk, Valkenburgh said, "They want to control who's in the hearing room. I'm going to send Mr. Gifford a telegram."

Mr. Gifford wired back: Stake out the courthouse.

The obvious problem for Roy Pickard and Oscar Young was how to have Albany Pelletier testify without exposing Charles Rich's lie about the time he was kicked by his horse. After the hearing was long over, Valkenburgh realized he'd been used by the lawyers to minimize Pelletier's testimony. Albany was one of the last witnesses to testify, only hours before the verdict was rendered, and Valkenburgh testified after Albany. Being a federal agent, he created a lot of excitement, which overshadowed anything Albany said. The previous Friday, a man named Ed Baldwin testified. He was a neighbor and friend of Rich's and a fellow Odd Fellow. Rich and Baldwin had a deal: Baldwin let Rich and his wife use part of his land for a garden, and the Riches let Baldwin use his barn and horse and buggy. On the night of the murder, Baldwin took Rich's horse and buggy out for a run. On Friday, April 18, Ed Baldwin testified the following:

PICKARD: What was the latest time you got back to Mr. Rich's house that night?

BALDWIN: Couldn't have been later than 8:45.

PICKARD: Couldn't it have been at nine?

BALDWIN: No, sir. I couldn't have used that much time unless I had walked the mare, which I naturally wouldn't do if I was out to give her a little exercise.

PICKARD: Was it as late as a quarter of nine when you were at Bean & Symonds for the sawdust? Supposing some person had said you were at Bean & Symonds at 8:45, just starting from there with the bag of sawdust, what would you say to that?

Baldwin: I wouldn't care to say very plainly just what I think of it.
Pickard: That you weren't there that late, you mean?
Baldwin: I wasn't there at that time, no, sir.
Pickard: Is there any doubt about that in your mind?
Baldwin: There is none, no, sir.

On the last day of the hearing, only hours before the verdict was read and after Pickard had interviewed Baldwin to bias the jury against any timeline that was not his, Albany Pelletier was called to testify briefly.

Pickard: Were you watchman at Bean & Symonds on the 13 of August, the day Mr. Dean was killed?
Pelletier: Yes.
Pickard: Did you see Mr. Rich's horse that night?
Pelletier: Yes, right down there by the sawdust chute.
Pickard: What doing?
Pelletier: He was doing nothing. He was tied up there to the post, and Mr. Baldwin was filling up some bags with sawdust. Ed Baldwin, it was.
Pickard: What time was this you saw him?
Pelletier: Nine o'clock at night, I saw him.
Pickard: How do you fix that time?
Pelletier: I go around every hour. I go once every hour, you know. I went at nine, and I would go again at ten o'clock, as you know. When I went around to see Mr. Baldwin, the clock was showing me nine o'clock.

Three hours later, the verdict came back: Dr. Dean was murdered by a person or persons unknown.

It was several years later, when people accommodated themselves to the verdict of the Grand Jury, that Russell and Susan Henchmen were sitting on their porch and the sky was getting dark from an approaching storm, and Russell told his sister he'd seen Mr. Rich when Susan stunned her brother:

"What people don't know is that Charles and I truly loved each other. Oh, I know there's twenty years between us, but he makes me feel like nobody else I've ever known. I didn't understand he was a prisoner of his accomplishments, and the reason he didn't leave Lana wasn't because of her, but because he was addicted to the respect and admiration the people had for him. If he left his wife for me, he would sully his prominent position, which he worked so hard to achieve, and because I didn't understand that, to get Charles's attention, I toyed with his emotions, which ended up in the killing of Dr. Dean. I will have that burden for the rest of my life.

"Charles is aloof, and it takes a lot to make him angry and his anger is violent when finally comes from somewhere deep inside him. I've seen him just turn and walk away from someone who's being difficult rather than risk having something really unpleasant happen. People think he's arrogant or rude, but the truth is, he doesn't want people to see his anger. The men around Charles, who admired and loved him, fixed it so he could live out the rest of his life knowing what a good man he truly was. I don't fault them one bit. Thirty years of good work and service to the community and society would take his life for one bad decision. Does that seem fair to you, especially since I was the one who teased him and taunted him by flirting with Dr. Dean?"

There was a clap of thunder and a flash of lightning. Russell tried to think of something to say.

Epilogue

The verdict of the Grand Jury has lasted over a hundred years. My title suggests there may be another explanation for what happened. I've used actual events from *Hearing by the Grand Jury on the Death of* William *K. Dean* by Margaret Bean, the daughter-in-law of Delcie Bean, and the Department of Justice reports, which I have fictionalized to get the greatest dramatic storytelling values. It was Margaret Bean who gave me several boxes of Department of Justice reports that she had released from the government under The Freedom of Information Act. The irony was she was an earnest Charles Rich supporter, and it was events recorded in these reports that encouraged and finally convinced me that the murder was not unsolved. Ultimately, it was the beauty of the story that kept me writing it for thirty years.

Charles Rich lived for another fifteen years and died in January of 1933, with a group gathered outside his home waiting for a confession. His wife, Lana, died five years later, and his sister-in-law, Georgiana Hodgkins, who didn't live in Jaffrey and died twenty-five years later, are all buried together. They are the only ones who know how Charles got his black eye. One can't help but think of an Eternal Pact.

Mrs. Dean died in September of 1919 while staying with Reverend Enslin.

Dr. Dekerlor died at the age of thirty-nine from a gunshot wound to the head in a Mexican bar. His wife, who he abandoned after she gave birth to a daughter, Elsa Schiaparelli, later went on to become an internationally known fashion designer on par with Coco Chanel, with clients like the Duchess of Windsor, Mae West, and Lauren Bacall.

The transcription of the Grand Jury testimony has an interesting history. Because there was no indictment at the end of the hearing, the stenographer's notebooks were stored away in the Keene Courthouse. The courthouse was refurbished in the late 1970s, and it was then that the workmen found the boxes of notebooks and evidence in a closet.

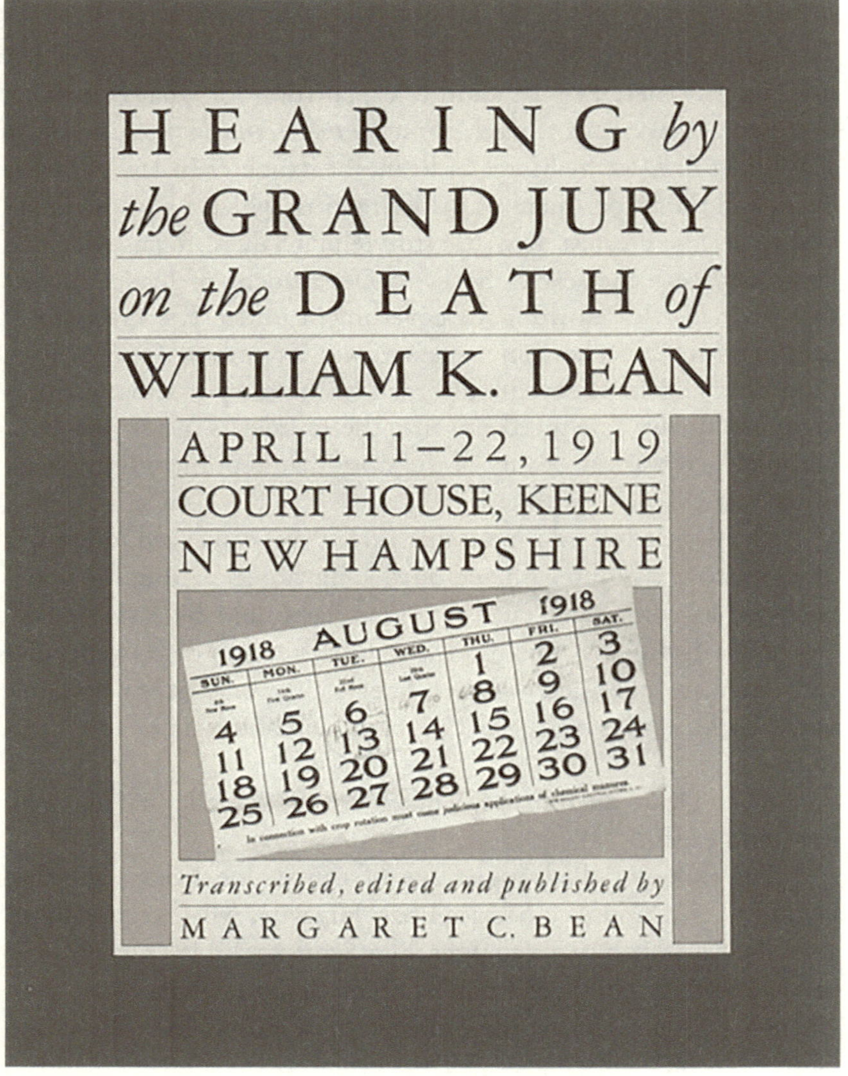

HEARING *by* *the* GRAND JURY *on the* DEATH *of* WILLIAM K. DEAN

APRIL 11–22, 1919
COURT HOUSE, KEENE
NEW HAMPSHIRE

Transcribed, edited and published by
MARGARET C. BEAN

When Margaret Bean heard about the stenographer's note-books, she asked the court if she could transcribe them. The court allowed her to take one notebook at a time, and when she transcribed that one, she could return it to the court with a copy of the transcription for the next notebook. The notebooks were in the Pittman shorthand, which luckily Margaret knew how to transcribe.

The End.

About the Author

Jack Coey has been studying and writing about the Dean murder, which happened 106 years ago tonight, for thirty years and is believed to be an unsolved murder. He has used the Grand Jury testimony and the Department of Justice reports to go back in time and has used those vehicles to investigate the investigation, which was a great deal of fun!

www.ingramcontent.com/pod-product-compliance
Lightning Source LLC
Chambersburg PA
CBHW022117150726
47990CB00003B/1393